*Summer Vacation
Devotions*

*By Tyrean Martinson*

Copyright © 2009 Tyrean Martinson

With Wings of Light Publishing

Createspace Edition 2015

Originally written for one-time use at Peninsula Lutheran Church

All rights reserved.

**Dedication**

Summer Vacation Devotions is dedicated to the Lord – Father, Son, and Holy Spirit.

Table of Contents

On the Road
    Packing and Planning
    At the Wheel
    Car Games
    The Map
    Rest Stops

At the Beach
    Water
    Sand
    Sunscreen
    Buckets of Treasure
    Sunglasses

Camping Out
    Tent Camping
    Flashlight Tag
    Campfire
    S'mores
    Summer Night Sky

About the Author

**On the Road**

**Packing and Planning**

"For I know the plans I have for you," says the LORD. "They are plans for good and not for disaster, to give you a future and a hope.'" Jeremiah 29:11 New Living Translation

When I was growing up, my dad did most of the planning, and almost all of the packing. After getting a family vote on a destination, my dad would be the one who figured out the mileage, the best time to leave, and all the exact details. Weeks before any camping trip, my dad would lay out all the camping gear on the basement floor to air it out and inspect it. He would plan meals, and make sure they fit in the packs we were taking.

When it came to packing, he packed everything except for everyone else's personal clothing or entertainment. Even in those departments, he gave guidelines. We didn't want to take too much. On a three week trip to England one year, we were allowed two changes of clothes, one book, a raincoat, a tooth brush, a bar of soap, shampoo, and the essential youth hostel sheets. Amazingly, I didn't mind, but I was eleven at the time.

When I met my husband, I was surprised at how much he could pack, if given the chance. When he went to Korea for a three week Navy reserve training one year, he packed two sea bags full of clothes. Just clothes! I guessed that he didn't want to wash any uniforms while he was there.

These days, I am the family planner and packer. Somehow, my dad's passion for vacation details has been passed down to me. I'm not detailed about much of my life, but on vacation, I want to have everything just right so I can relax with no worries. I reserve hotels, plan snacks and meals, make an itinerary with built in "do-nothing" days, and write packing lists. I chase my kids around the house, and inspect their bags to make sure they've packed enough socks and their swimsuits. I pack my husband's clothes as well as mine.

So what in the world does this have to do with my relationship with God? Well, essentially, I have a hard time giving him the plans. I have a hard time trusting God to pack the right things for me, and to make the right plans. A few years ago, one of my long-term plans for my life went awry, and I struggled in my relationship with God. I was angry with the situation, and angry with God's plans not matching mine. I had to re-think things. I had to trust God in a new way, and it was tough. It was tough because I had to give up my plans for God's plans. I had to trust God to pack my heart with enough love, strength, and wisdom to move forward on my lifetime journey.

During that time, this verse reminded me to trust in the only trustworthy planner. "'For I know the plans I have for you,'" says the LORD. "'They are plans for good and not for disaster, to give you a future and a hope.'" Jeremiah 29:11

During that time of frustrated plans, I kept asking God for a clear direction, and he's been nudging me ever since. "Whether you turn to the right or to the left, your ears will hear a voice behind you, saying, 'This is the way; walk in it.'" Isaiah 30:21 NIV

Many of us like making our own plans, but when God gives us a clear direction we can't ignore it. I invite you to join me in asking God for that clear direction, and then trusting in Him.

Prayer: Awesome God, Creator of the Universe, Savior of our souls, Spirit who dwells within in us, guide us on your paths, lead us in your direction, and give us the strength to trust in you alone. Amen.

**At the Steering Wheel**

A long time ago, I used to be "THE Driver". I drove my friends everywhere, and didn't let anyone even touch the radio controls in my car. I drove for the fun of it. I drove and loved it.

These days, I'm in the passenger seat on long trips. I wonder how it happened sometimes, except I know my husband is even more passionate about being "THE Driver" than I am. He is a little easier than I am in some areas. I get to change the radio stations, put in different CDS. I can even fiddle with the heat and AC, although I noticed that he changes them back to his favorite settings a few minutes after I'm done.

The driver doesn't have to be the ultimate planner for the vacation, but he/she does have the controlling vote on when we stop and where; if you've ever had a child ask repeatedly if the driver would just pull over for a quick rest stop break and had the driver continue on past two rest stops, you know what I mean about this.

This brings me to God as the driver of our lives. Even if we are passionate about driving ourselves, God steps in and takes the wheel. He is in charge. Maybe he plans more rest stops for us than we originally planned to take. Maybe he plans a longer drive than we intended. I just know for certain that God takes the wheel even when we don't give it up.

Our lives are generally easier when we give the steering over to God right from the beginning of our trip. Each day, each morning, when we turn our lives over to him, he gives us rest, he makes our burdens light. He gives us strength for the journey. He loves us enough to lead us beside still waters.

God is the driver of our lives, as he is our shepherd. As Jesus states in John 10:14-15: *"I am the good shepherd; I know my sheep and my sheep know me—just as the Father knows me and I know the Father—and I lay down my life for the sheep." (NIV)*

The Lord is a shepherd we can trust, so let's let him drive us on our journeys through life.

Prayer: Psalm 23

*"The Lord is my shepherd, I shall not*
*be in want.*
*He makes me lie down in green*
*pastures,*
*he leads me beside quiet waters,*
*he restores my soul.*
*He guides me in paths of*
*righteousness*
*for his name's sake.*
*Even though I walk*
*through the valley of the shadow of*
*death,*
*I will fear no evil,*
*for you are with me;*
*four rod and your staff,*
*they comfort me.*

*You prepare a table before me*

*in the presence of my enemies.*
*You anoint my head with oil;*
*my cup overflows.*
*Surely goodness and love will follow*
*me*
*all the days of my life,*
*and I will dwell in the house of the*
*Lord*
*forever."*
*Amen.*

**Car Games**

Miles rolling by, green on green, as we drive away from reality into vacation. Tired by road food, we doze sleepily. Then it happens, the miscommunication that turns into laughter. Then we lapse into silence. We listen to the rattle of a soda lid in a cup holder. A call for new music, and we have the whine of electric guitars and violins, with passionate vocals. We play 20 questions, with more than 20 questions. We find the alphabet forwards and backwards on license plates. A few arguments occur and we take break, get snacks, and get back in the car.

"Are we there yet?" is a question that we all want to avoid hearing when we are on a long car trip, and yet it seems inevitable. This question, tied with the statements, "I'm hungry" and "I'm thirsty" seem to be timeless.

Just take a peek at Exodus.

Exodus 16:2-3 *"In the desert the whole community grumbled against Moses and Aaron. The Israelites said to them, 'If only we had died by the Lord's hand in Egypt! There we sat around pots of meat and ate all the food we wanted, but you have brought us out into this desert to starve this entire assembly.'"*

Exodus 17:2 *"So they quarreled with Moses and said, 'Give us water to drink.'"*

Throughout Exodus, Numbers and Deuteronomy, the Israelites continue to complain, and it all seems to meld into that age-old question, "Are we there yet?" For their rebelliousness and grumbling, God gives them a 40 year journey in the desert. Thankfully, I haven't been on any car trips that have lasted that long.

Trips of any kind take patience, perseverance, and preparedness. This trip that we are on, from birth to heaven could be up to 120 years. Only God knows how long our journey will be, but he's give us ideas of how to journey.

"Rejoice in the Lord always. Again, I say: Rejoice!" Philippians 4:4

Remember, this letter was written by Paul, who persevered through shipwrecks, imprisonment, and long trips during his ministry.
This kind of rejoicing is found down deep in our hearts, where the Holy Spirit is working on us.

Galatians 5:22 *"But the fruit of the Spirit is love, joy, peace, patience, kindness, goodness, faithfulness, gentleness and self-control. Against such things there is no law."*

There are many scriptures that teach us how to live, and how to journey. We can go to God's Word any time to find the fruits of the Spirit in action.

Prayer: *Awesome God, Creator, Redeemer and Holy Spirit, praise be to you for all wonder and joy! Lord, we ask that you fill our souls with your joy, and give us all that we need for this journey of life. Amen.*

**The Map**

B.I.B.L.E. – Basic Instructions Before Leaving Earth

Picture yourself sitting in the passenger seat, the AC fanning your face, and the golden blue sky of summer just outside the window. Suddenly, the driver wants our attention. He wants to know how many miles it is to the next possible gas station, or where the next turn off is. We have to pull out the map. Sometimes it's buried beneath coloring books, journals, and CD's. We might not have looked at in miles, and now when we need it, it's hard to find amidst all the junk food wrappers and entertainment we've been using to keep our car trip interesting.

Finally, we find it, creased, folded wrong and stained with cola or coffee. Unfolding it to find the right part is sometimes an ordeal, with it flopping around in our laps, and the driver becoming increasingly insistent that we find the information they need and find it fast. Somehow the map turns upside down, and then we get it the right way . . . finally. We find where we are, and find our destination. We get the directions, follow them, and the map gets passed to our kids in the back seat who want to see where we've been and where we're going. It's a teachable moment. Geography, Cartography, and a few Biblical truths all held in a wrinkled old map. And maybe it's not our kids in the backseat, maybe it's grandkids, grandparents, friends, or cousins who've come on the road trip with us. It doesn't really matter. It's still a teachable moment.

Is this the moment when we regale our family or friends with stories about treasure maps? Maybe.

I think it is the time to give them the greatest story ever told, which also happens to be the greatest treasure map of all time. Only in this treasure map, the "X" that marks the spot is in the shape of a cross. That's why Christmas gets called "Xmas" because that "X" represents the cross. Jesus is the greatest gift, and a relationship with the Lord through Jesus' redeeming love is the treasure that lasts through eternity.

Check out these treasure map directions, straight from the treasure map itself:

Proverbs 2:1-5 NLT
*My child, listen to what I say,*
*and treasure my commands.*
*Tune your ears to wisdom,*
*and concentrate on understanding.*
*Cry out for insight,*
*and ask for understanding.*
*Search for them as you would for silver;*
*seek them like hidden treasures.*
*Then you will understand what it means to fear the LORD,*
*and you will gain knowledge of God.*

Isaiah 33:6
*"He (God) will be the sure foundation for your times,*
*a rich store of salvation and wisdom*
*and knowledge;*
*the fear of the Lord is the key to*
*this treasure."*

John 3:16 *"For God so loved the world that he gave his one and only Son, that whoever believes in him shall not perish but have eternal life."*

John 6:68 *"Simon Peter answered him, 'Lord, to whom shall we go? You have the words of eternal life.'"*

Eternal treasure is found in the greatest map of all time, the Bible. Let's look for the cross that marks the spot.

Prayer: *Awesome God, Creator, Savior, and living Spirit, guide us as we seek your treasure that you have stored up for us in your word. Amen.*

**Rest Stops**

Weary from the road, tired from sitting in the same position for hours, we stumble from our cars onto a patch of green. We've pulled into a rest stop, a place where we can stretch our legs and aching backs. We wake ourselves from the haze of driving with strong coffee or a soda, or maybe just a quick jog on cement paths. We debate taking out our Frisbee, or maybe we walk our dogs. Then we look at the large, posted map with that wonderful arrow pointing at "you are here." With our kids asking questions, we talk about where we've been, and where we're going, and reflect on the journey so far and the journey ahead. Within a few minutes to an hour, we are rested and re-energized, ready for another long drive. We've been to a rest stop.

Whether you like to take car trips like many Americans, or whether you fly to your destinations, God gives us many opportunities to rest in Him. For example, right at the beginning in Genesis 2:2, the Bible states,

*"By the seventh day God had finished the work he had been doing; so on the seventh day he rested from all his work. And God blessed the seventh day and made it holy, because on it he rested from all the work of creating he had done."*

So we have a built in rest stop each week. Every Sunday morning, we can stumble into our church, stretch our aching minds, and wake from the haze of driving through our hectic lives with praise in song, food for our souls, and reflection on the journey behind and the journey ahead.

I would like to invite you to come and take a rest stop at worship each week on even on your vacations. If you stop at a rest stop this summer, take a moment and think about or discuss what it means to rest in God's presence.

There are many great verses that speak directly about rest in God's Word, and here are just a few of them to take with you on your journeys this summer:

Jeremiah 6:16a
*"This is what the Lord says:*
*'Stand at the crossroads and look;*
*ask for the ancient paths,*
*ask where the good way is, and walk*
*in it,*
*and you will find rest for your souls.'"*

Exodus 31:14 *"The Lord replied, 'My Presence will go with you, and I will give you rest.'"*

Prayer: Psalm 62:1 *"My soul finds rest in God alone; my salvation comes from him."* O Lord, awesome God, Prince of Peace, Holy Spirit, I thank you for the rest you have given me, and I ask that you help me seek rest in your Word this day. Amen.

**At the Beach**

**Water**

When we're at the beach, we dip in our toes, gaze at the waves, skip, and play catch me if you can with the ripples rushing onto the beach. Standing there, it pulls our feet down into the sand. We splash it. We run in it. Walk with our toes just touching it.

The ocean is a favorite spot for our family. Traveling to see the wind and the waves, to feel the tidal pull beneath and between our toes as we sink into the sand, is a joy to each of us. One year when we didn't travel to the ocean – the "real ocean with waves and wind," my oldest daughter told me that it wasn't a complete summer. "Like summer didn't happen all the way," she said. We missed it, and yet we live in a place blessed by the water, in rain, lakes, rivers, and Puget Sound beaches. But still, we miss the coastal ocean with its giant waves, chilling to the touch.

Water – cool, refreshing, beautiful, relaxing. When waves lap or pound on the shore, we feel as our souls are being soothed by the rushing water. Our worries are carried away. Water is a source of renewed life, and relaxation.

Water is wonderful, but even more so when God is in clearly enters in.

In Exodus 15, the Israelites were thirsty and they needed water. They needed good water, not just any kind.

Exodus 15:22-25 *"Then Moses led Israel from the Red Sea and they went into the Desert of Shur. For three days they traveled in the desert without finding water. When they came to Marah, they could not drink its water because it was bitter. (That is why the place is called Marah.) So the people grumbled against Moses, saying, "What are we to drink?"*

*Then Moses cried out to the Lord, and the Lord showed him a piece of wood. He threw it into the water, and the water became sweet."*

When God enters in, bitter water is made sweet, and life-giving.

*"Jesus answered, 'Everyone who drinks this water will be thirsty again, but whoever drinks the water I give him will never thirst. Indeed, the water I give him will become in him a spring of water welling up to eternal life.'"* John 4:13-14

So when we are wading in the waves this summer, let's think about how God has given us sweet, life-giving water that cleanses and renews our souls.

Prayer: *Awesome God, maker of all good things, cleanse us with your life-giving water, and renew us with your waters of eternal life. Amen.*

## Sand

Sand, hot underfoot, shifts beneath us as we walk and run across the beach. We throw ourselves down onto the sand, and run it through our fingers, try to hold it in our hands and watch it seep through the cracks of our fingers. At the water's edge, we enjoy its coolness against our hot feet, and kneel to make sand castles.

We pile up the walls with buckets and hands, and scoop out our moat. In the center we build our castle. We dream big, imagining sculpted towers, and crenellated walls. However, in my family we never bring those kinds of tools. We use our buckets, our hands, pieces of shells, sticks, rocks and seaweed to build up our creation. It sags with too much water, or too little.

Sometimes we look at it with disappointment, but that quickly gives way to joy as we fill in the moat, and begin to make up adventures that might happen at our castle. We capture tiny crabs and put them in our moat, watching them bury themselves deeper into the sand to escape our attentions.

Every moment is wonderful, and we love the feel of the sand, both dry and wet, on our hands, and under our knees as we play.

Then our attention wanders, and we decide to bury Daddy up to his knees in wet sand, or play catch-me-if-you-can with the waves lapping on the shore. We find other pursuits, and come back later to find our castle. This proves to be a hard task. The castle is no longer there, but only lumps of sand, half-covered with the tide. Which lumpy castle is ours?

The moment of realization that our castle, our hard work and effort, is gone is usually one that includes some sadness. Even when we know it's going to happen, we hope somehow that the tide will spare our little creation. When we've built farther from the water's edge, we've found that our castles still fall apart, or eventually get washed away by the tide. Even sand castle contestants must face the temporary nature of their art work.

This crucial moment, when we realize that our sand crafts will melt away with the tides, or be blown away by the wind, is where we can find a lesson from God in our lives. First, we can acknowledge that He is forever, where the earth is only temporary. Then we can dive into one of Jesus' teachings, from the book of Matthew.

*"Therefore everyone who hears these words of mine and puts them into practice is like a wise man who built his house on the rock. The rain came down, the streams rose, and the winds blew and beat against that house, yet it did not fall, because it had its foundations on the rock. But everyone who hears these words of mine and does not put them into practice is like a foolish man who built his house on sand. The rain came down, the streams rose, and the winds blew and beat against that house, and it fell with a great crash."* Matthew 7:24-27, Jesus' parable.

Prayer: *Lord, creator and redeemer, give us the wisdom to build our lives on you, and your Word so that we can stand firm with you for all eternity. Amen.*

**Sunscreen**

It's that time of year, when we all smell like . . . sunscreen. I admit that sunscreen is probably my least favorite part of summer. Dutifully, I put it the white, gooey stuff because it protects my skin from cancer. Modeling good behavior, I put it on in front of my kids. My husband is always the first one to get it out and the last one to put it away each year. With sensitive, easily burned skin, he needs it just to be able to enjoy a summer day without pain.

When we go to the beach, with the light reflecting off the water, sunscreen is even more important. So, we layer it on, more than once a day. Most families might use SPF 30, but with my husband and youngest daughter, SPF 50 or higher is used in our household. So sunscreen is a necessity. As it we rub it on, it becomes invisible, and we can only smell its lingering scent.

Like sunscreen, we have protection from God. Unlike sunscreen which is like sticky chalk, God's protection is like armor. Even though it soaks into our souls and isn't visible to the eye, God's protection shines in our daily walk with God.

*"Therefore put on the full armor of God, so that when the day of evil comes, you may be able to stand your ground, and after you have done everything, to stand. Stand firm then, with the belt of truth buckled around your waist, with the breastplate of righteousness in place, and with your feet fitted with the readiness that comes from the gospel of peace. In addition to all this, take up the shield of faith, with which you can extinguish all the flaming arrows of the evil one. Take the helmet of salvation and the sword of the Spirit, which is the word of God."* Ephesians 6:13-17

So, at the beach this summer, or wherever you are putting on sunscreen, try to imagine that you are putting on God's armor too. As you put it on your arms and shoulders picture that belt of truth and the breastplate of righteousness. When you put in on your legs and feet, think about fitting your feet with the readiness that comes from the gospel of peace. Then, as you rub it all in, think of that shield of faith. As you put in on your face and neck, think of that helmet of helmet of salvation, and the sword of the Spirit. I know that if I can do that this summer, putting on sunscreen might be cool.

Prayer: *Awesome God, thanks for your amazing armor that you have given us through your Word. Thank you for your salvation, your righteousness, and your faith. In Jesus' name we pray. Amen.*

**Bucket of Treasures**

Have you ever carried a bucket, sloshing with water, up the beach to make a vacation home for crabs? Or used a bucket full of salty water to wash colorful rocks and iridescent shells?

Digging through the sand to find buried treasures of amazing rocks, scuttling crabs, and rainbow hued shells is one of my favorite beach pastimes. I'm newly amazed each trip by the sparkles in the rocks, and the amazing color combinations. Feeling the rough edges that give way to smoothness makes me think of how God is smoothing the rough edges out of my life.

As a child I wanted to bring home buckets and pockets full of these treasures. My parents limited the amount of sandy booty that I brought home, but after more than thirty years of digging up buried treasures, I've managed to fill a few windowsills with them.

These days however, we've all learned that the delicate balance of the beach's ecosystem is a good reason to not bring any of the treasures home. I face a dilemma every time I'm at the beach. I yearn to bring home a piece of sandy treasure. Yet, I feel that honoring God's creation by being a good steward and taking care of His creation is a way that I can honor God. For me, environmental concerns are spiritual concerns. God made this amazing, wonderful place that we live, and our purpose is to worship him, and honor him. When I do bring home treasures from the beach, I limit myself and I pray that God renews and redeems the earth and all that live here.

The dilemma over bringing home beach treasures brings to mind the dilemma we all have over earthly treasures of any kind. In Matthew 6:19-21, Jesus states, *"Do not store up for yourselves treasure on earth, where moth and rust destroy, and where thieves break in and steal. But store up for yourselves treasures in heaven, where moth and rust do not destroy, and where thieves do not break in and steal. For where your treasure is, there your heart will be also."*

So as I stand on sandy shores this summer, I plan on thinking over those verses as I enjoy the simple treasures of shells, rocks, and sand. What kinds of treasures do I have? And where do I store them? I invite you to think over these questions too.

Another scripture describing this heavenly treasure is 1 Timothy 6:18-19, *"Command them to do good, to be rich in good deeds, and to be generous and willing to share. In this way, they will lay up treasure for themselves as a firm foundation for the coming age, so that they make take hold of the life that is truly life."* Goodness, good deeds, generosity, and willingness to share (the good news) are all ways of storing up heavenly treasure. So let's ask ourselves, what treasure will God find in our lives?

Deuteronomy 26:18 *"And the Lord has declared this day that you are his people, his treasured possession as he promised and that you are to keep his commands."*

Prayer: *Awesome God, Creator and Redeemer of the heavens and earth, and all who dwell on the earth, we give thanks and praise to you for declaring that we are your treasure. We ask that you give us the wisdom and the ability to store up our treasures in your heavenly stronghold, and not on earth. Thanks and Praise to you, Jesus, our treasure. Amen.*

**Sunglasses**

"The future's so bright, I gotta wear shades" Timbuk 3

Those lyrics run through my mind almost every time I put on sunglasses. It's an old 80's tune, not Christian, and yet I still love that line and that tune. I find myself humming it in my car, on the beach, wherever I'm wearing shades. My husband sings it with me. Our kids laugh at us, and we laugh at ourselves.

So what do sunglasses have to do with going to the beach, or with the Word of God? Well, we often wear sunglasses to the beach on a bright day. They protect our eyes, and help us focus on the fun we're having without needing to squint. The shades protect my eyes from the sun, but what if when I put them on, I think about my eternal future? Is it going to be bright?

Revelation 21:23 (NIV) states, "The city does not need the sun or the moon to shine on it, for the glory of God gives it light, and the Lamb is its lamp."

If that doesn't sound bright enough for sunglasses, think about Revelation 21:25, "On no day will its (the city's) gates ever be shut, for there will be no night there."

There will be no night in the city of God, and God's glory will give it light, and the Lamb (Jesus) will be its lamp. That sounds incredibly bright.

To find out how bright God's glory might be, just think how it was reflected on Moses' face in Exodus 34:29-30, "When Moses came down from Mount Sinai with the two tablets of the Testimony I his hands, he was not aware that his face was radiant because he had spoken with the Lord. When Aaron and all the Israelites saw his face was radiant, they were afraid to come near him."

Plus, God did create the heavens and the earth, and the first thing he created was . . . light. "And God said, 'Let there be light,' and there was light." Genesis 1:3

Now, let's find out about Jesus, the Lamb being the lamp in the city of God. In John 8:12, "Jesus said, 'I am the light of the world. Whoever follows me will never walk in darkness, but will have the light of life.'"

There are around 65 references to light in the Bible. So next time you put your shades on, think of the future brightness of God's heavenly city and try to remember one of those scriptures.

Prayer: Awesome God, creator of light, light in our hearts and light of the world, help us remember how bright our future is in you. Lord, we ask that you shine your light through us and into the lives of others around us. Thanks and Praise to you alone, our savior. Amen.

**Camping Out**

**Tent Camping**

The wonder of tent camping – the musty old tent smell, the hard ground cushioned inadequately with thin cushions or cold air mattresses that pull the heat from our bodies and send it to the ground. And yet, there is something about the experience of tenting that is more exciting and fun than sleeping at a hotel, or in a camper.

My kids insisted that we do some tent camping one year. First we tried it in our backyard, with coyotes howling just on the other side of our fence. Then we went for a four day tenting trip on the Olympic Coastline. We set up the tent in the dark, and had pouring rain greet us for breakfast. With blue tarps, and ropes over tree limbs, we found some dry spaces, just in time for the sun to come out. The girls loved it. They loved the tent, sleeping in sleeping bags all bunched together. They wanted to play in the tent during the day, and at night.

Living out of a tent is exciting and fun, but most of us agree that we wouldn't want to live out of one forever, right?

We have to remember that these earthly homes where we live – these bodies, our houses – are like tents compared to the kingdom of God that awaits us in heaven. That's something that gives me pause. Everything we have now is like a musty smelling, squashed, hard ground tent in comparison to the glory, and majesty of heaven.

2 Corinthians 5:1-5
*"Now we know that if the earthly tent we live in is destroyed, we have a building from God, an eternal house in heaven, not built by human hands.*

*Meanwhile we groan, longing to be clothed with our heavenly dwelling, so that what is mortal may be swallowed up by life. Now it is God who has made us for this very purpose and has given us the Spirit as a deposit, guaranteeing what is to come."*

John 14:2 (Jesus says) *"In my Father's house are many rooms; if it were not so, I would have told you. I am going there to prepare a place for you."*

So while we enjoy our camping trips this summer, and revel in the fun of tent camping, let's think about how amazing our Father's house is going to be when we get there. Jesus himself is preparing us rooms.

If you want to read about an "ultimate" camping trip, just check out Exodus. The Israelites camped in the desert for 40 years. Then read Luke 1-2, and think about how Jesus left the amazing glory of heaven to be born on earth in a stable, and "tent" with us in humanity. Wow! He loves us a lot.

Prayer: *Awesome God, lover of our souls, we praise you for your creation! We praise you for your heavenly glory, and we look forward to dwelling there with you. Thanks for saving us! Amen.*

## Flashlight Tag

Psalm 119:105 (NRSV) "Your word is a lamp to my feet and a light to my path."

Flashlights are fun. They shine bright circles on a tent's walls; they shine beams into the darkness, and flicker over the ground as we walk. They light our way in darkness, and help us find our way. We can even play games with flashlights. Have you ever played flashlight tag?

In a game of flashlight tag, having the flashlight beam light you up, means you are it, you have been tagged.

I think this I think it's been played since God created the world, and he started with light.

Genesis 1:3 "And God said, 'Let there be light,' and there was light."

Then Jesus keeps the game going in the New Testament.

In John 8:12 "When Jesus spoke again to the people, he said, 'I am the light of the world. Whoever follows me will never walk in darkness, but will have the light of life."

So we have an amazing, awesome God who created light, and who is light, and then –

Matthew 5:14-16 "You are the light of the world. A city on a hill cannot be hidden. Neither do people light a lamp and put it under a bowl. Instead they put it on its stand, and it gives light to everyone in the house. In the same way, let your light shine before men, that they may see your good deeds and praise your Father in heaven."

So God creates light, Jesus is the light, and then "tag, you're it," you (we) become the light. And it happens just that fast. When we immerse ourselves in God's word, we get tagged by God's light, and Jesus' love shines through us into our everyday lives. When we're tagged, we don't have to think about being "it", we just are . . . it's part of the game, and it's how God works in and through our lives.

When God makes us His light in this world, we simply have to keep in his word, and keep showing up in our everyday lives. People will notice the light and ask us about it. Then, that's the tricky part . . . making sure we direct them to the source of light and life. Then, "tag, they're it," happens to them, and the light keeps shining on in the darkness, beams growing and crisscrossing until dawn breaks anew.

John 1:1-4 "In the beginning was the Word, and the word was with God, and the Word was God. He was with God in the beginning. Through him all things were made; without him nothing was made that has been made. In him was life, and that life was the light of men."

Prayer: Amazing Creator, Light of the World, Holy Spirit, we praise you! Shine your light in and through our lives so that darkness is overcome wherever we go. Amen.

**Campfire**

2 Corinthians 3:18 "And we, who with unveiled faces all reflect the Lord's glory, are being transformed into his likeness with ever-increasing glory, which comes from the Lord, who is the Spirit."

Light flickers against the darkness, bringing light to our faces, and warmth to our toes. We build it up, and flames rise up towards the sky. The campfire draws us like moths, for warmth, for light, and for the companionship that takes place around it. Stories are told, games are played, dinner is made and treats are toasted as we gather together around the campfire.

Before we can enjoy all that the campfire gives us, we have to build it up carefully. Not everyone's dad brings a torch to light the fire, so we gather twigs, moss, and kindling. Newspaper and paper plates make good fire starters too. The first fire in the campfire pit that is lit every trip is done by my husband. He lets the girls and I start to build it up, and then he jumps in, adds more kindling here and there, placing everything just right, and finally lighting the match. The flames flicker to life, and we feed them until they blaze into a merry source of heat, light, and fellowship.

A relationship with God is like that campfire. We build it up slowly, piecing together the right materials, and placing them in the right spots. Even if we have been Christian our whole lives, we sometimes need to rebuild a fire of faith after, or during, a storm. So we gather the dried kindling in prayers, Biblical study, and worship. We place them in our lives weekly, then daily, finding just the right times and spots for them. Then God, who has been there the whole time already, lights the flame of faith in our lives. The flame flickers to renewed life and light, and we can draw near to the source of life, light and fellowship in our lives . . . our Lord, and savior, redeemer and refiner.

> Zechariah 13:9
> "This third I will bring into the fire;
> I will refine them like silver
> and test them like god.
> They will call on my name
> and I will answer them;
> I will say, 'They are my people,'
> and the will say, 'The Lord is our
> God.'"

Prayer: Awesome God, refiner and redeemer, we praise your holy flame that burns in our lives. We thank you for your refining fire, and your Spirit that shines through our lives. Amen.

**S'mores**

Ingredients
Marshmallows
Chocolate Bars
Graham Crackers
Roasting Sticks
A Bible
An open heart

Directions
- Read the Bible passages first.
- Then discuss while roasting marshmallows over the campfire.
- Break Graham Crackers into halves, place ¼ to ½ chocolate bar onto ½ Graham Cracker.
- Place roasted marshmallow onto the chocolate bar.
- Put second half of the Graham Cracker on top, and squeeze the marshmallow off your roasting stick, until you have an awesome marshmallow, chocolate, graham cracker sandwich, or s'more.
- Note: Do not attempt to read Bible passages after roasting s'mores – your fingers will be too sticky.

Most of us know how to make s'mores, but did you know that you can get recipes for them off the internet? I've been making them around campfires for as long as I can remember, and after 8 years in Girl Scouts plus many years of experience, I've tried every variety of s'more that I can think of – raw, slow-roasted, medium well, liquid, blackened (Chicago style?), and with a varying amounts of chocolate.

The gooey sweetness of a well-roasted s'more dripping around the edges of the graham crackers is one of the best treats around the campfire. No matter how you like them roasted, or how much chocolate you use, the taste is almost like heaven. In fact, I think that God gave us our taste buds to remind us of his heavenly grace. Think about it. God made us so that means he made our taste buds. We can use our sense of sweetness to remind ourselves of God's sweetness.

> Psalm 119:103
> *"How sweet are your words to my taste,*
> *sweeter than honey to my mouth!"*

Isn't this true? God's word is sweeter than anything, even s'mores.

> Proverbs 24:13-14
> *"Eat honey, my son, for it is good;*
> *honey from the comb is sweet to*
> *your taste.*
> *know also wisdom is sweet to your*
> *soul;*
> *if you find it, there is a future hope*
> *for you,*
> *and your hope will not be cut off."*

God's wisdom is sweet to our souls. Amen.

> Proverbs 16:24
> *"Pleasant words are like a honeycomb,*
> *sweet to the soul and healing to the bones."*

Isn't this so true? When we use pleasant words with others around us, healing takes place in our relationships, and they become sweet in a lasting way.

The sweetness of God's wisdom, God's word, and Godly relationships last for eternity. So when that s'more taste has melted off your tongue, hang on to the sweetness of God that lasts forever.

Prayer: *Lord, Creator of all things sweet and wonderful, we praise you for our sense of taste. We praise you for your word, your wisdom and your sweet love that heals our souls. Amen.*

## Summer Night Sky

Job 38:4-7
*"Where were you when I laid the*
*earth's foundation?*
*Tell me, if you understand.*
*Who marked of its dimensions?*
*Surely you know!*
*Who stretched a measuring line*
*across it?*
*On what were its footings set,*
*or who laid its cornerstone—*
*While the morning stars sang*
*together*
*and all the angels shouted for*
*joy?"*

Gazing at the night sky has become a rare, relaxing past-time for many of us. On those few occasions when we are out far enough from city lights to see the night sky, we are caught in awe and wonder. There is the sense of smallness of our own lives, and a sense of the vastness of God's universe.

Whether we pick out constellations or make up new ones, we are amazed by the vast scope of God's universe, and are struck by a sense of almost timelessness. The world around us may be moving fast, but the night sky seems almost still. God is steady and unchanging. He is in charge of all of the universe – the stars, the sun, our planet, our individual lives – and he cares for each of us deeply.

Psalm 8:3-5

*"When I consider your heavens,*
*the work of your fingers*
*the moon and the stars,*
*which you have set in place,*
*what is man that you are mindful of*
*him,*
*the son of man that you care for him?*
*You made him a little lower than the*
*heavenly beings*
*and crowned him with glory and*
*honor."*

"I am the Alpha and the Omega," says the Lord God, "who is, and who was, and who is to come, the Almighty." Revelation 1:8

Daniel 12:3 *"Those who are wise will shine like the brightness of the heavens, and those who lead many to righteousness, like the stars forever and ever."*

Genesis 15:5 *"He (God) took him (Abram) outside and said, 'Look up at the heavens and count the stars – if indeed you can count them.' Then he said to him, 'So shall your offspring be.'"*

I invite you to wonder anew at God's love for us, and his care in every detail of our lives and our universe.

Prayer: *Lord, O Lord, how majestic is your name in all the earth! Creator, Savior, and Living Spirit, renew our sense of wonder at the work of your hands. Amen.*

**About the Author**

Tyrean Martinson has taught Sunday School for too many years to count, served on church councils in the past, and been asked by Pastors to give lay sermons and consider seminary. With a full plate of homeschooling, teaching, writing, and reflection on God's Word, Tyrean has opted for following God's directions, letting Jesus take the wheel on the peaceful hazy summer days, the stormy dark nights, and the sunset drives into the horizon.

If you are interested in homeschool writing curriculum for teens, Tyrean Martinson is working on a Dynamic Writing series which will be partially released in 2015 with subsequent books coming out in 2016 and beyond.

If you are interested in fiction reading, Tyrean has a Christian Fantasy trilogy for young adult and adult readers called *The Champion Trilogy*. The series is action-heavy, so please note that it is meant for readers who can handle reading scenes which include injury, sword-fighting, battle scenes, and death. The characters in the series must rely on faith to see them through their troubles, and prayer is emphasized.

For more information about Tyrean Martinson and her work, you may find her online at:

Tyrean Martinson, Every Day Writer
http://tyreanswritingspot.blogspot.com/

Amazon
http://www.amazon.com/Tyrean-Martinson/e/B00BCKPHZK/

Facebook

https://www.facebook.com/TyreanMartinson

Also, please note that Tyrean writes books in several genres including secular speculative fiction which has a bit of an edge. Tyrean hopes that these other works will lead people to read her Christian titles and ask about the one true hope that is present in her life – Jesus.

**For every book sale of Summer Vacation Devotions, Tyrean Martinson will give her earnings to benefit Peace Rehabilitation Center in Nepal to fight human trafficking.**

Made in the USA
Monee, IL
19 June 2020

34179585R00031